Addition, Addition, Subtraction

A work of
Nicolas Abdallah

To a _truly good_ friend.

1

cover and interior art by Nicolas Abdallah

www.somewhatbrief.com

ISBN 978-0-557-09618-3

Printed in the United States of America

"Consider it pure joy, my brothers, whenever you face trials of many kinds, because you know that the testing of your faith develops perseverance. Perseverance must finish its work so that you may be mature and complete, not lacking anything. If any of you lacks wisdom, he should ask God, who gives generously to all without finding fault, and it will be given to him."

James 1: 2-5

For my lovely wife, thank you.

The "strangers along the track", thank you.

Introduction

At the age of sixteen my world fell apart. My parents separated. The aftermath of this haunts me to this day, seven years later. The separation was intense and confusing for me. My father had been abusing my mother for years and in an effort to protect herself and her children she did what she thought best, ask him to leave. My father walked out of my life and abandoned our relationship, leaving me to pick up the pieces of my broken heart. I have wrestled for many years to understand why he abandoned me. On my journey of healing I have pondered much, cried much, and learned much.

This book is a compilation of poems and short essays that I have written throughout the years. They document my struggle to understand the choices that my parents made and where that left me.

I have found great comfort in my personal faith, a faith in Jesus Christ which I force upon no one, but a faith that has been crucial to my personal journey.

1

I can see the coast line,
moving towards me at the speed of light.
swimming in the sands of time,
swirling and spinning through my blank mind.

There's an old man,
he's searching for the Promised Land.
Thinks he'll find it in a soda can,
only bruised from falling back to earth.

It's in dreams we come alive.
In dreams we find our place.
In dreams we feel our worth.
When we grasp out towards to sun.

I can feel the cool breeze,
it's running from the crashing waves.
colliding with a freight train,
sending embers into the horizon line.

There's a young girl,
she's searching for the Promised Land.
Thinks she'll find it in a razor blade,
only scarred falling back to earth.

It's in dreams we come alive.
In dreams we find our place.
In dreams we feel our worth.
When we grasp out towards to sun.

I can see the coast line,
moving towards me at the speed of light.
swimming in the sands of time,
swirling and spinning through my blank mind.

There's a young man,
he's searching for the Promised Land.

2

Fell asleep in a digital existence,
woke to a pounding inside my brain.
I can't remember what your words meant,
it's all a blurry photograph.

Finding joy inside molten sand,
formed by an artist hand.
It brings peace like a sunrise,
and makes the moonlight dance.

See those lights in the distance?
Soon you'll be back home.
Living life in a tape-deck,
rewind, playback, rewind.

3

Jumped aboard a runaway train,
nothing but clothes in my pack,
don't know where it's going,
North and South are the same to me.

Momma always said be weary of strangers,
said they could steal the clothes off your back,
said the sun in the east will blind you,
said the sun to the west will abandon you,
said the moon will stab you in the back.

I've seen miles and miles of pain and heartache,
my heart is heavy and spirit is broken.
I'm bitterly cold and have been stripped naked,
my only friends have been strangers on the track.

.yearnings.

In the fall of 2008, my wife and I were driving from Tennessee to New York to visit with family. I am unsure whether it was the length of the drive or lack of sleep, but for some reason I started to think about my father and how I would love to talk to him. I could picture it vividly, us sitting in a booth at a tiny restaurant in Phelps, New York. A restaurant that I had met my father at many times before.

I felt no anger towards him, no bitterness in this moment. I felt like a young child yearning for his fathers embrace and that little pat on the back that is so often taken for granted. I have never had such a vivid experience before. Unfortunately, I did not act upon these feelings and call him while we were in New York. I was scared and hesitant of being rejected and hurt again by another let down.

The father that I missed was the dad who threw a baseball back and forth with me until dark. The father who taught me how to do simple repairs around the house and sparked my curiosity to learn how things worked. The father I missed was the dad who would give me a smile and a nod from the other side of the fence when I made great plays for my baseball team. These are my yearning moments. It did not hit me until that long drive that these moments of yearning should not to be passed up. They are the little kid inside of me screaming, "I want my father!" I should embrace them. They are the most innocent part of me speaking out.

Many times in college, I broke down in the arms of my girlfriend because I wanted so badly to play catch with my dad. I would have loved to go back to those moments when my father was working on projects and I would sit there and admire him, hoping that someday I would be half the handy-man he was. He truly was my hero of the home fix-it projects.

Often times I would brush off these thoughts as moments of weakness for myself. I had to be strong because if I was not I would get burned. It has taken me many years to understand that these are not moments of weakness, they are moments of greatness. If there is anytime in my life that I am being real, it is when I am yearning for the things that make me feel like I am a son and I have a father who loves me. In hiding from these moments I am denying myself the possibility of healing.

I am reminded of an even more recent moment where I was brought to tears. My wife and I were watching a television show about a superhuman nanny from the UK. The story began by explaining that this family was separated and the parents were looking at getting divorced. As the story was beginning to unfold it went to a "confession cam" of the young child in the story. I do not remember exactly what was said by this young child but I know that tears began to flow down my face because I had felt exactly every word that this child spoke. My wife graciously turned the channel and I thanked her. In this moment I wished that my relationship with my father was worlds different.

No more hiding. Embrace innocent yearnings.

4

Analog in a digital world,
your voice is a dial tone,
from a mobile phone.
Etched into the call log,
I'd decline your call,
If I knew what was good.

I'd cut these wires,
If I knew what was good.
The wires that connect
you and me.

Pen and paper in a digital age,
your words are Morse code,
from a laptop computer.
Marked read in my inbox,
I'd block your address,
If I knew what was good.

I'd destroy this circuit,
If I knew what was good.
The circuit that connects
you and me.

If I knew what was good,
I'd stay the hell away.
There are too many,
wires between you and me.
If I knew what was good,
I'd turn and look away.
There are too many,
connections between you and me.

But the truth,
the truth is.
I know what is good.
But I still long,
long for.
Connections between you and me.

5

We are the patchwork, defined
by beauty and possession.
We are the method, the machine
and the madness that keeps us moving.
We are the king and queen divided,
the kingdom we built with blood and sweat.
We are the crown on our heads,
the anointed ones that share no burdens.

Yet, life slips through our cracked hands.
The words on our lips; the sharpest of knives.
The strength in us, used for destruction's bliss.
Angels weep over us and demon's rejoice.
We are the cursed, the damned.
We are Blasphemy and Hypocrisy.
We are utterly human.

In all of the blindness,
the fog and mire we wander.
In all the failure and murdered dreams.
In every broken promise,
and crooked intention.
We are utterly human.

We are utterly Loved.

<u>6</u>

I've tried to forget you in so many ways,
tried to delete you from time and space.
Pencil to the paper, erasing the lines,
it's going to take a life time to scratch
the ink from the page.

.felt-board father.

I never imagined that five words could send me into an emotional roller-coaster, somewhere between irritated and completely lost. "Let God be your father." I have heard these words too many times to count. First of all what an incredibly difficult concept to grasp, God being someone/something residing in the invisible and my father being someone that is flesh and bones. Secondly, I could not believe that God was capable of such a thing. I felt that He obviously did not care too much about me, my family was in shambles. What kind of God would take my father away? What kind of God would allow me to feel so abandoned? I know that this phrase was stated with the best of intentions, but my father was "dead" and I had no idea where to begin the grieving process let alone to think about how God could fill this void. So, I did not think about it. I continued to let anger settle in and fill the chasm inside.

The first step for me was to develop my personal relationship with God. This proved to be a slow process as I found that I did not really know who He was. The beautiful thing about God is that He seeks you out, He is never far, and He will not abandon. Over time God was faithful to heal wounds and mend the broken pieces. However, I still found myself wondering how He was going to completely fill the void left by my father. I wondered how He was going to meet the physical needs that I had, the need for a warm embrace and the need to play catch. I was not sure how he was going to do this but I was willing to give Him a chance.

The funny thing about God is that he speaks when we are not listening and acts when we are not looking. I was so blind, I did not see that He was already filling this void, the whole time I was doubting His ability to do so. He was patting me on the back in the flesh and bones, with amazing male role models that He had placed in my life. He was playing catch with me through great friends and afternoon pick up games. He was more flesh and bones than I had given him credit for. The body of Christ is very visible and very real, and He will use anyone within, in very real ways. I have no idea what any of the male role models thought about me upon first meeting me or what God may have been placing upon their heart. What I do know is that it was wonderfully purposeful and beautifully orchestrated by the hands of God because He knew what I needed.

<u>7</u>

You are a scurvy salesman,
a master of your trade.
Selling guilt and blind allegiance,
sewing anger in your wake.

I've always stood up for the flaws,
never questioned imperfections.
Put my neck on the block for you,
blind loyalty until the end.

No longer can I purchase,
the snake oil that you sell.
No longer will I wander,
behind your hollow shell.

The depression, it's moving in,
like a cold and steady wind.
From your hills of bitterness,
to the valley, my soul within.

The depression, it's rolling in,
like a cold and steady fog.
From your towers of destruction,
to the valley, my soul within.

<u>8</u>

Etched into the still frame,
our silver-chloride memories.
Trapped between white borders,
happiness smothered tragedies.
I have a photo box for a brain,
full of self made false securities.

I've tried to store them in the basement,
but they always resurface in the light.
I've torn you out of photographs,
but know i'll always miss that piece.

Seems every shot I framed of you,
was picture perfect and imaginary.
I'd love to see a real photograph,
no more color coated melodies.
I'd love to see a real photograph,
like you walking out on me.

<u>9</u>

Twisted and torn,
my stomach it churns.
Getting my hope up is dangerous,
i've got scars from the burns.

I'd scream it out loud,
if you weren't miles away.
I'd scream it out loud,
but you never listened anyway.

Held hostage by a child,
just yearning for a hug.
I'd give just about anything,
for one true moment of love.

I'd scream it out loud,
if you weren't miles away.
I'd scream it out loud,
but you never cared anyway.

<u>10</u>

I can't seem to cross the gap,
fragments and sparks,
a misfire of the synapse.

Your words cut the line,
between reality and
what's jumbled inside.

Just can't quite spit it out,
just can't make sense,
of any of this.

.dial-tone from a mobile phone.

Disapointment is nothing new for me, but it seems that every time it is a little bit different. Recently I have taken a more introspective approach. A search for meaning as to why as much as it hurts, I keep running back. What compels me to try again, when it seems failure is inevitable? Why is it so hard to forget him? What makes deleting his number from my phone so difficult?

He is not an old friend, he is not a passing acquaintance, he is my father. I was not wired to forget him, as he played a part in creating me.

We had been out of contact for about a year when I began speaking to my father again. Part of me has been jumping for joy because it wanted that connection and part of me was screaming, "run like hell and do not look back."

For the first couple of weeks I felt great about being in contact with my father and it was great to catch up with him. Then Christmas came. Through our conversations my father knew that my wife and I were going to be in New York for the holiday, but made no effort to ask about getting together. I also learned while in New York that my siblings had been invited to his parents house and no invitation had been extended to us. I was extremely hurt. The feeling was nothing new but for some odd reason I was surprised. For some reason, reality and truth had become blurred through my childish eyes and I allowed myself to get hurt.

The life long dilemma unfolds, do I go with what I know to be true and what I know about my father and his relational abilities or do I walk blindly as a child into hurt? In almost every other aspect of life it seems that the truth precedes all else. How long will I be locked in this state of childhood ignorance, when can I just grow up and discard this relationship that any intelligent person would because it is so volatile? I am tired of wishing that he would pat me on the back and tell me he is proud of me and then be surprised when he does not. I just want to break the connection, but it seems impossible. His voice is a dial-tone from a mobile phone, out of place, but I can not stop taking his call.

11

I'm writing You this song,
a reminder of the things,
You already know.
A melody floated,
on the waves of time.
You set me in motion,
know my deepest thought.
How great is Your patience,
How wondrous Your love,
A contract tested,
hour by hour.

It's the ebb and flow,
only the ocean knows.
It's the re-occuring chance,
I always take for granted.
It's the reset clock,
only the maker knows.
another chance,
another morning glow.

It's a crooked thought,
a common mistake,
but You already know.
I doubted Your judgement,
Your unfailing ways.
You set me in motion,
know my darkest deed.
How great is Your patience,
How wondrous Your love,
A contract tested,
hour by hour.

It's the ebb and flow,
only the ocean knows.
It's the re-occuring chance,
I always take for granted.
It's the reset clock,
only the maker knows.
another chance,
another morning glow.

12

A deal with the devil,
between anxiety and fear.
Setting storms into motion,
sea tossed soul, darkness draws near.

A slow motion film,
I see you walk away from me.
Replayed in my mind,
over and over, constantly.

Today I broke the chains,
the bonds of captivity.
A child held hostage,
by yearnings inside of me.

More than a conqueror,
destined to be set free.
No cell can dare to hold,
A soul in the hands of Thee.

13

Your grace never ceases to amaze,
how silence can be so marvelous,
how tears can be a cleansing rain.

.unashamed.

I have never been one to easily open up and share, I tend to hold my thoughts and feelings inside and often times bury them very deep. It is not a healthy habit, I admit, but it is what I have learned to do. For the longest time I did not believe I had a voice, or at least that anyone would want to listen to what I had to say.

It is hard to remember the first time I shared about my experience with father absence but I can recall the most liberating moment. It took place during a Family Systems class during my undergraduate work. The topic was grief, and I had been wanting to speak up for sometime. I began by sharing that I was experiencing a sort of grieving process in my own life. My father was not dead but I was grieving his absence. I shared with the class that it was a difficult process because if he was dead there could be finality in the process eventually. However, the fact that he was living seemed to perpetuate the cycle of grieving. I distinctly remember that following the class a fellow student approached me and simply said, "thank you for having the courage to share." It meant a lot to hear, and was a turning point for me. My experience meant something to others. I knew from this moment on that I could no longer be silent.

It is incredible how our journeys intertwine and our experiences are not so different. I recently received a message from a church member who had read a poem that I had posted to a social networking site. She stated that she could relate to what I had written. I am uncertain on what level she could relate but that is not of importance. The fact is that words have great power and I was slowly finding that God wanted me to share the great things that he was doing inside of me, the struggles and the triumphs.

I know that God has allowed me to experience these trials because he knew that I could handle them. Most of all He knows that with a little bit of work, He can use my brokeness and transform it into something beautiful.

14

The soil it seemed so fertile,
the task appeared to be futile.
We schemed in new paragraph's,
working delicately from photograph's.

Ones and zero's into the ground; sown,
The harvest reaped; our own.
It was a well thought out plan,
a well executed and strategic stand.

Packaged in electronic flight,
Seems it was met with immediate disgust,
was the fruit we sent, bitter to the touch?

The soil appeared to be fertile,
the task it seems so futile.

<u>15</u>

I won't understand the way You look at me,
must be beauty in chaos,
must be beautiful inadequacy.

<u>16</u>

Distract me from the valley oh God,
keep my eyes fixed on Your purpose.
For where my eyes are set,
there my feet will walk.

The murderer is set to slay me,
his words a beautiful poison,
his lies a bitter deceit.

Oh God You are a crown upon me,
oh God You are my passion.
For where my eyes are set,
there my feet will walk.

17

Take me deeper oh Wonderful one,
lead me further oh Glorious one,
I'm tired of this cycle,
I'm tired of the shallow end.

.tunnel vision.

It was only a matter of time before the pain made its way to the surface. For too long I had been burrying all of my feelings and emotions deep within. My freshman year of college was my great escape from home and the bondage it seems existed there. I felt liberated and ready to make my own mark. What I did not realize was that before I could be free, I had a lot to work out.

As the school year progressed I began to fall deeper and deeper into depression. The root of it being that I felt so defeated by the relationship with my father and the constant ups and downs. I had been extremely let down a number of times and it was beginning to take it's toll on my mind and body. Although I had been exposed to the suicide attempts of my own parents, I had not thought of suicide up until this point in my life and had never self-harmed.

As the pain began to build and I began to bury it deeper and deeper, it became so unbearable that I had to find a way to release it. That is when I cut for the first time, I felt like I was in a tunnel and it was getting longer and longer, the light was dissipating at a rapid rate. I have never felt such lonlieness in my life before, as though there was no one who would care one little bit about me. By God's grace my girlfriend entered my dorm room at this point, came over and wrapped her arms around me and I bawled. I can not imagine what she must have felt at this moment, we had not been dating for very long but I thank God that she was in my life and still is today.

Burying is a dangerous habit, I learned the hard way that it is incredibly important to find ways to release emotions in a healthy manner. I personally have found great comfort in writing poetry. It seemed easier at the time to hold inside the anguish and pain that had been inflicted by my father, but I paid the price in the end.

18

Have you ever been abandoned?
Have you ever been let down?
Their mouths form a canon,
words shell your lonely town.

Have you sat in a dark place?
Have you cursed your mortal soul?
Their motions like a circus,
acting only for the show.

Have you dreamed of heaven?
Have you planned your escape?
Their hands are unblemished,
never touching soil or the spade.

<u>19</u>

I cannot imagine life without you,
my chest an empty lot.
You are the song that brings life,
a living melody throughout my veins.

Countless time you've picked me up,
shattered pieces; heart and soul.
Your love seems never ending,
a soundtrack He knew I would need.

20

The glow is seeping in,
filling the dark spaces.
I've been a wanderer too long,
seeking light in dark places.

Illuminate this shell,
it's been veiled too long.
enlighten this soul,
it's been despondent too long.

The glow is seeping in,
filling in the dark spaces.
Soon this hollow,
will be something beautiful.

<u>21</u>

Oh how we hide our dark,
below a crooked sun,
and a sea of glass shards.

22

Must have missed your call,
I swear you said you would.
Oh God I need Your grace,
my mind is a tempest,
my mouth will soon follow suit.
It's a mysterious letdown,
a perplexing nonevent.
My heart is torn of two colors,
a spineless yellow,
and an ill-tempered red.

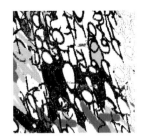

I am picking up these nails,
cutting down that tree.
Today I am building a bridge,
O God please support me.
Too long I've tried to cross this void,
with devices of my own creation,
methods of my own demise.
Today I look to the sky,
with every clang of this hammer,
I feel closer to reaching the other side.

24

The sun rises and sets,
no regard for your first and last breath.
Gravity does not bow to your command,
it only pulls you closer to death.

How insignificant your mortal frame,
from dust it came and shall return.
A holding cell, a prison,
your soul trapped within.

Cursed from the moment you breathe your first,
with sinful pleasure to the right and the left.
What God should expect good of this?
What Heaven could hold such wretched wanderers?

Must be grace abundant ocean waters,
waiting at the gates of life.
Must be memory erasing super computers,
ready to wipe your murderous past.

Must be grace abundant ocean waters,
waiting at the gates of life.

It is difficult to truly describe feeling abandoned. The pain of deciet and disapointment. I have been lost in this desert for quite some time, I have seen the mirage and, regrettably, hoped. When he walked out that the door that last time my parents tried to make it work, I knew it was over. I knew that he was not coming back. I knew it was the last chance I had for him to be my father. The abandonment slowly but surely led to depression for me and just when I thought the world could not close in on me any further, I found purpose.

Finding purpose in life is not completed with a ten step guide. I did not wake from sleep to "purpose" smacking me in the face. It took breaking down, almost completely, finding the valley and slowly making my way towards higher-ground.

I found purpose in pain and suffering. Destruction and tragedy were pieces of the puzzle, parts of my personal journey. I could have easily given in and given up, many times thoughts of doing so plagued my mind. I could have found solace in drugs, numbing the pain with each inhale and exhale. I often wonder why I did not choose such exits. It would have been easy to open those doors and never look back.

I believe that God has placed a purpose on my life as He has quite evidently sparred my life a time or two, I shouldn't have walked away from a car wreck a few years ago. I have found that everything I have experienced has always been turned into something good. God allowed me to experience my fathers absence knowing that I could turn it around and share it with others, providing support and empathy.

.feeling abandoned, finding purpose.

Oh merciful God,
how faithful You are.
You see state of my heart,
the whole, the light and the dark.
How many times I have denied You,
How often I have cursed Your name.
Oh merciful Saviour,
how gracious You are.
You see the state of my heart,
the hole, the need and the dark.

26

A short wave radio canvas,
paint your individual collapse,
it's a singular scene,
we'll pretend we're all listening.

It's a break in dialogue,
it's our own damn fault,
it's a bi-polar transmission,
something we'll blame on someone else.

27

You worked so hard,
only to become what you've always hated.
Swore that with your last breath,
you'd break the pattern, yours to bear.
I've been in your shoes,
I've seen what you have.
We've walked the same path,
shared the same fears.
A difference exists,
between you and I.
The past and present,
became your future.

28

Is God on the inside or out,
if He's on the outside then,
tell Him to please come in.
I've been speaking for weeks,
words can't seem to break the clouds.
Maybe you can attach my words,
when you send yours through.
I promise it's an important message,
not just a frivolous list of gripes and moans.
Is my transponder broken?
Did the valley consume me?
Maybe you can attach my words,
when you send yours through.

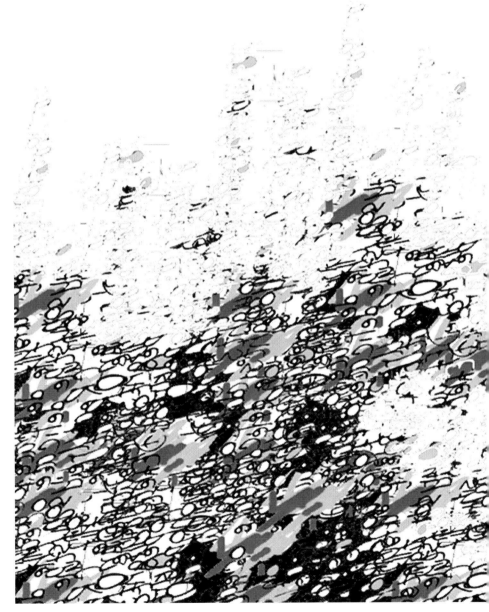

29

He that gives,
provides abundantly.
Taking freely,
never more than can be lost.
Addition,
Addition,
Subtraction.

www.somewhatbrief.com